Baseball

 **YOU** ...are the manager
...call the shots

Michael Teitelbaum

A *Sports Illustrated For Kids* Book

First Edition

Library of Congress Cataloging-in-Publication Data

Teitelbaum, Michael.
    Play Book! You're the manager : you call the shots—baseball /
by Michael Teitelbaum.—1st ed.
      p. cm.
    "A Sports Illustrated for kids book."
    Summary: The reader as coach calls the plays in this baseball game
and then flips pages to see the outcome.
    ISBN 0-316-83624-9
    1. Baseball—Miscellanea—Juvenile literature.   2. Baseball—
Managers—Miscellanea—Juvenile literature. [1. Baseball—
Coaching—Miscellanea.]   I. Title.   II. Title: You call the shots—baseball.
GV867.5.T45   1990
796.357—dc20   89-48218
                                               CIP
                                             AC

SPORTS ILLUSTRATED FOR KIDS is a trademark of
THE TIME INC. MAGAZINE COMPANY.

Sports Illustrated For Kids Books is a joint imprint of Little, Brown and Company and Warner Juvenile Books. This title is published in arrangement with Cloverdale Press Inc.

10 9 8 7 6 5 4 3 2 1

BP

For further information regarding this title, write to Little, Brown and Company, 34 Beacon Street, Boston, MA 02108.

Published simultaneously in Canada
by Little, Brown & Company (Canada) Limited

Printed in the United States of America

Interior design by Aisia de'Anthony

Illustrations by Donna Nettis

This book is dedicated to Sandy Koufax, my first sports hero. To the 1986 New York Mets, for all the thrills. To the neighborhood Mets fans, for the pizza, the friendship, and for rooting the loudest. And to my wife, Sheleigah, for always being in the seat next to me for all the Mets games (even if they're only on radio).

I would like to thank my editor, Richard Amdur, for his help in the shaping of this book.

ATTENTION!

*All reader-players must read this page
before the start of today's big game!*

How many times have you watched a baseball game and thought, "What a dumb decision that manager made! What he *should* have done was . . ." Well, that's what this *interactive* book is all about.

There is an important ongoing baseball game taking place in this book, and as the manager of the home team, *you* must look at all the choices you have as the game goes on, make your own decisions and see what happens as a result. In this way, you don't read straight through as you would do with a regular story. Instead, each of your decisions will lead you to a new situation and eventually affect the outcome of the game.

Should you send the runner with the pitch? Should you play your infield in? Do you stay with your starting pitcher or bring in a relief pitcher? It's all up to you.

Follow the directions at the bottom of the page to guide you to the choice you want. At the end of the game, you can go back to the beginning of the book and try some different options. It will be a whole new ball game, because there are 25 different endings to the game! In some you win, in some you lose. How the game turns out is entirely up to you. So, play ball! Put on the old baseball thinking cap and get ready to guide the home team to victory!

OFFICIAL ROSTER

Your Team: *(You choose the name!):* _____

Manager *(Fill in your name or the name of your favorite manager):* _____

Your Key Players:

Starting Lineup		Position	AVG.	HR
1	Rob Burns	CF	.310	2
2	Guy Diego	RF	.280	14
3	Chris Freeman	3B	.267	20
4	Al Berico	LF	.247	30
5	Patrick Berry	2B	.255	12
6	Judd Jackson	1B	.271	4
7	John Miner	SS	.231	2
8	Pedro Gonzalez	C	.256	11
9	Mark McAndrews	P	.114	0
	or			
9	Bombo Torres	P	.138	0

Pinch Hitters		AVG.	HR
Ben Mooney (righty)		.308	4
Brent Moore (lefty)		.277	1

Pinch Runner		AVG.	HR
Lee Wilcox		.218	2

Pitchers	W-L	ERA	IP
Mark McAndrews (lefty starter)	18-6	2.59	223
Bombo Torres (righty starter)	21-12	3.10	217
Ron Murphy (lefty reliever)	6-1	1.96	94
Freddie Dunn (righty reliever)	5-3	2.35	80

The Announcer: _____

(Pick the name of your favorite announcer— from TV, radio or even your own neighborhood. Whenever you read the announcer's words in Play Book! Baseball, *imagine the announcer you picked as saying them.)*

RBI	SB	Notes
44	38	Good base stealer
51	15	Rookie—has started all season
77	7	Steady veteran—solid offense and defense
91	16	Struggling with average, but has good power
60	10	Great defensive player
54	9	Has only average speed, but is an aggressive, intelligent base runner
9	1	Just up from the minors
50	1	Excellent defensive catcher; slow runner
2	0	Strikes out a lot; hits into many double plays
10	0	Has gotten some clutch RBI hits this season
17	2	Seasoned veteran; best pinch hitter in the league this year
12	5	Rookie; good speed on bases
9	15	Great speed and baserunning ability

SO	BB	Notes
91	56	Finesse artist, can paint corners with breaking stuff
185	70	Blazing fastball, effective curve, slider, changeup
88	40	Ace of the bullpen; 21 saves
42	30	Great sinkerball; 16 saves

Starting Lineup for the Pennville Protons

		Position	AVG.	HR
1	Steve Malley	2B	.299	3
2	Carlos Ferrer	CF	.305	7
3	Sam Alexander	3B	.268	10
4	Luis Acosta	RF	.260	39
5	John Neff	1B	.280	28
6	Trevor Nelson	LF	.240	14
7	Nick Klein	C	.261	11
8	Walker Smith	SS	.256	4
9	Woody Campbell	P	.145	0

Pitchers	W-L	ERA	IP
Zeke Wilson (righty starter)	17-10	3.22	206
Snipe Conley	7-5	1.95	74

Your Opponents: The Pennville Protons

4

RBI	SB	Notes
39	32	Great speed
48	11	Good bunter
34	10	Rookie
106	4	Leads the league in home runs, but has been in a slump for the last 10 games
89	11	On a hot streak for last 15 games
50	7	Good outfielder, but does not have a great arm
49	0	Strong arm, but sometimes throws wild
40	9	Has made a lot of errors this season
6	0	Strikes out a lot

SO	BB	Notes
88	71	Good variety of pitches, can be overpowering at times, but can also be wild at times
80	25	Blazing fastball, but has given up 4 game-winning home runs; 32 saves

This is a big game, a really *big* game. I know, I know, they're *all* big games. That's what they tell you your first day in the minors. But this one is different: it's the biggest game of the season. Here we are, tied for first place with the Pennville Protons on the last day of the season. We're playing the Protons, who've had a steady grip on first place for the last two months, at our home ballpark. If we win today, we win the division and head for the playoffs. It's that simple.

Our club has been in first place for a total of two days—yesterday and today—and that covers the last six seasons. The best finish we've had was third place two years ago—but then we dropped right back down to fifth last year. This year, in July, we were eight-and-a-half back! And now, here we are, all tied up. The whole season comes down to this one game.

If you had told me two years ago, when I was managing in Triple A ball down in the minor leagues, that today I'd be managing a team in the National League, well, I would have said that you were nuts. And now, to be skipper of a team that's one game away from making the playoffs? Forget it. I mean, *nobody* picked us!

There were people who thought I wasn't ready to manage in the big leagues. "He's too unorthodox," they said. "Plays too many hunches," the newspapers said. I admit, I don't always play by the book. But sometimes I just get a feeling in my gut, and when I do, I go with it. Besides, it keeps people on their toes. I like keeping people on their toes.

This whole town's going nuts, too. The newspapers

have been running "Pennant Fever" headlines, and the fans have been packing the ballpark for the last month. Today's game has been sold out for a good two weeks.

I've got faith in my guys. It's been a long, tough season, but they came together at just the right time. Rob Burns, my centerfielder, has been hitting the ball well all year, and lately he's been tearing it up on the bases, too. And I couldn't ask for more from my rookie rightfielder, Guy Diego. He's hitting a solid .280 in his first full season. We're strong at third base with Chris Freeman and at catcher with Pedro Gonzalez—two steady veterans. Both of them are fielding well and having decent years at the plate with steady batting averages. My first baseman, Judd Jackson, isn't that fast, but he always hustles. Nothing I like to see more than a ballplayer who hustles!

We're strong in the middle of the infield, too. Patrick Berry, my second baseman, has been a Gold Glove winner for years, and though the kid at shortstop, Johnny Miner, who we just brought up from Triple A, is still learning how to hit, he has great range and instincts. Of course, my leftfielder, Al Berico, is my power man. His average is down this year, but not enough to move him out of the cleanup spot, batting fourth. I feel good about these guys. Real good.

It's not going to be easy, though. We'll be playing another fine ball club. The Protons made it to the World Series two years ago, and are in the driver's seat again. That rightfielder of theirs, Luis Acosta, can hit the ball a country mile, and he's leading the league in home runs. The team as a whole has good speed, good power and excellent skills. Their centerfielder, Carlos Ferrer, batting second, is a good bunter who can hurt you if you don't watch out.

In our pitching rotation, I would normally start my

righty fastballer Bombo Torres today, but the Protons entire lineup is packed with good fastball hitters. I could go with my lefthanded finesse artist, Mark McAndrews. The Protons would have more trouble hitting his fancy stuff—but then again, he'd be starting out of turn, and might not be as sharp.

Hey, the whole season's on the line! Do I go with my well-rested fastballer, Torres, against a good fastball-hitting team, or do I send out McAndrews, my finesse pitcher, on only three days' rest?

▲ *To start the righty fastballer, turn to page 10*

▲ *To start the lefty finesse artist, turn to page 12*

9

*H*i, everybody, and welcome to today's game. I'm your personal play-by-play announcer, about to bring you all the action and excitement of this important National League game on the last day of the regular season. It's a beautiful day for baseball. We can see a few high clouds drifting by, but there's absolutely no threat of rain. A gentle breeze is blowing from rightfield to leftfield, rippling the flag a bit, but it's not strong enough to affect fly balls today. If anyone's going to hit one out, he'll have to do it with his own power.

Speaking of power, there's plenty of it here in the ballpark this afternoon. The Protons' rightfielder, Luis Acosta, leads the league in homers with 39, and their first baseman, John Neff, has been on a tear for the last three weeks, batting .366 with 10 home runs and 21 runs batted in.

You've got some power in your lineup, too, and a great deal of power on the mound today. Your righty fastball pitcher, Bombo Torres, will start, taking his regular turn in the rotation.

The stadium is packed with fans. You can hear the noise building already, feel the electricity in the air as your team takes the field. Listen to that crowd! Torres is on the mound, taking his warm-up tosses. He's had a terrific year, already a 20-game winner, with a record of 21-12, a 3.10 ERA, and 185 strikeouts—the third highest total in the league.

Stepping in to lead off is the Protons second baseman, Steve Malley. Batting .299, he has three home runs and 39 RBIs. He's stolen 32 bases this year and is one of the quickest men in the league. Here's the big righthander's windup and the pitch. . . .

It's grounded back through the box. Johnny Miner, the shortstop, dives and . . . snags it. It's going to be tough to get this speedy man at first. Miner gets to his feet, now here's the throw . . . Malley is safe, for an infield hit. Miner made a dazzling play just getting to that ball, but with such a speedy runner charging down the line, Miner had no chance to make the throw to first.

*J*ust what I didn't need—the Protons leadoff man on base. There's so much they can do now. They can try a straight steal, a hit-and-run, or try to bunt him over. Their centerfielder, Carlos Ferrer, is up next, and he's a good bunter. My gut feeling is he's gonna bunt.

If I play for the bunt,I can have my first and third basemen charging on the pitch. But if I don't hold Malley on first, he can take a big lead and possibly steal on me. Maybe I should just pull my third baseman, Chris Freeman, in to the edge of the infield grass to guard against the bunt, and have my first baseman, Judd Jackson, hold the runner.

▲ *To bring your third baseman in and have your first baseman hold the runner, turn to page 14*

▲ *To have your first and third baseman both charging for the bunt, turn to page 16*

11

*H*i, everybody, and welcome to today's game. I'm your personal play-by-play announcer, and I'll be bringing you all the action and excitement of this important National League game on the last day of the regular season. It's a beautiful day for baseball. We can see a few high clouds drifting by, but there's absolutely no threat of rain. A gentle breeze is blowing from right field to left field, rippling the flag a bit, but it's not strong enough to affect fly balls today. If anyone's going to hit one out, he'll have to do it with his own power.

Speaking of power, there's plenty of it here in the ballpark this afternoon. The Protons rightfielder, Luis Acosta, leads the league in home runs with 39, and their first baseman, John Neff, has been on a tear for the last three weeks, batting .366 with 10 home runs and 21 runs batted in.

On the mound today will be your lefthanded finesse artist, Mark McAndrews, pitching out of turn on three days' rest. We've got to believe that this was one of your famous gut feelings. The Protons have got a great fastball-hitting team, so you've decided to throw your finesse pitcher at them, hoping he can outfox them, even though he's not as rested as you'd like him to be.

The stadium is packed with fans. You can hear the noise building already, feel the electricity in the air as your team takes the field. Listen to that crowd! McAndrews is on the mound, taking his warm-up tosses. He's had a terrific year, and is one of the real standout lefthanders in the league, with a record of 18-6, which gives him the best winning percentage in your rotation.

And his 2.59 ERA is in the top five for National League starters.

Looks like we're ready to start. Stepping in to lead off is the Protons second baseman, Steve Malley. Batting .299, he has three homeruns and 39 RBIs. He's stolen 32 bases this year and is one of the quickest men in the league. The crafty lefthander goes to work on him....

He walks Malley. Of course, this speedster is not someone you like to see on base. What's this? Here comes the manager out to the mound. Well, he's certainly not wasting any time in putting his unorthodox managing style into effect visiting the mound so early in the game. He's meeting with the entire infield out there.

I've got a hunch, guys. Their next batter, Carlos Ferrer, is a great bunter. I'm sure he's going to lay one down the third base line. I'd like to get that jackrabbit Malley off the basepaths. Maybe the third baseman should try to cut down the lead runner at second if we see a bunt.

What's that? I know, he's so fast that there's a chance we won't get him at second and then they'll have two men on with their big guns coming up. Uh-oh, here comes the ump to break up this little tea party. We've got to decide how to play it.

▲ *To try for the lead runner at second, turn to page 18*

▲ *To play it safe and try for the man at first, turn to page 20*

13

With Malley safe on first, next up is the center-fielder, Carlos Ferrer. He's had an outstanding year at the plate, batting .305, with seven home runs and 48 RBIs. He is such a skillful bunter, I think everyone in the stadium is expecting him to lay one down.

Malley takes his lead a few steps off first base. John Neff, the first baseman, holds the runner. Third base-man, Chris Freeman, inches up until he's just at the edge of the infield grass, looking for the bunt.

Your pitcher, Torres, comes to the set position, checks the runner on first. Here's the pitch . . . Ferrer squares to bunt. He lays one down the third base line. Here comes your third baseman, Chris Freeman. He makes the bare-handed pickup, then throws back across his body going for the runner at second. It's a great throw. Here's the slide, the tag . . . Malley is . . . *out!* Out at second on a spectacular play by Freeman! He fielded the ball cleanly and then fired it back in time to get the speedy lead runner out at second.

Now the Protons have a man on first, and one out. Ferrer is not nearly as fast as Malley, but he has stolen 11 bases this year. The infield is back at double-play depth, with the first baseman, Jackson, holding the run-ner. The next batter is rookie third baseman, Sam Alex-ander, who takes two called strikes and then swings and misses for strike three. This brings up the league's lead-ing home-run hitter, Luis Acosta, who hits a towering fly ball to deep leftfield. It'll stay in the park, however, as your leftfielder, Al Berico, gets under it and makes the catch to end the inning.

In the bottom of the first you'll be facing their super righthander, Zeke Wilson, who is 17-10 this year with a 3.22 ERA, 88 strikeouts and 71 walks. He's got a good variety of pitches, including a nasty slider, an 88-mph fastball and a very effective changeup. He can over-power hitters with his hard stuff, but he can also be wild at times. If he's in control, he's awfully hard to beat.

Your centerfielder, Rob Burns, leads off. A textbook leadoff hitter, he's batting .310, with 38 stolen bases. The pitcher, Wilson, is into his motion. Here's the pitch . . . he bunts it between the first baseman and the pitcher. No one is going to get to this one in time.

All right! I love that guy leading off. Robbie does all the things a leadoff hitter should do—doesn't strike out much, draws a lot of walks. He's really the catalyst of our offense. And talk about a smart hitter. He didn't get any signs from me; he was bunting all on his own. I guess I'm not the only one on this team who plays hunches.

O.K., my rookie rightfielder, Guy Diego, is up next. Should I try a steal or a sacrifice? Diego's not a great bunter, so maybe I should send the runner. But they'll be expecting Robbie to steal, so the bunt might catch them by surprise.

▲ *To try to steal second, turn to page 22*

▲ *To try to sacrifice bunt, turn to page 24*

*T*he Protons leadoff man, Malley, is on first with an infield single. That brings up the centerfielder, Carlos Ferrer. He's a .305 hitter who is the best bunter on this team.

Malley takes a big lead off first. Bombo Torres, working from the stretch position, brings his hands to the belt and checks the runner on first. He steps off the rubber and throws over—Malley gets back easily. Now Malley steps away from the bag, and Torres resumes his motion.

Your first and third basemen both charge down the line, looking for the bunt. Ferrer squares to bunt, then pulls the bat back and slaps the ball over the head of the charging first baseman for a base hit to right. Malley is digging for third. He'll get there easily with that tremendous speed. The throw comes in to second. Malley and Ferrer are safe, thanks to that crafty hit by Ferrer.

*S*on of a gun! I have to admit that's smart baseball. Ferrer went up there thinking bunt, but when he saw my first and third basemen charging, he pulled the bat back and popped one over the first baseman's head. Now they've got runners at first and third, nobody out.

We've got to go to double-play depth in the infield, but what should I do with my outfield? The Protons have their rookie third baseman, Sam Alexander, coming up. Our scouting reports say this kid, who bats right, is strictly a pull hitter, slapping the ball over to left throughout his whole minor-league career. This year he comes into the majors and now they're trying to teach him to go the other way, to rightfield. When I saw this kid play in the minors, all he ever did was pull. Down there the outfield would shift over as though it was on automatic. But with the work he's done this year, he could cross you up and send it the other way.

Should I play the outfield straight, assuming he has learned to hit to right, or should I shift the outfield for the pull hit?

▲ *To play the outfield straight away, turn to page 28*

▲ *To put on the outfield shift, turn to page 30*

That brings up their Number 2 hitter, centerfielder Carlos Ferrer. He's a fine hitter, batting .305 this year, with seven home runs and 48 RBIs. He's also an excellent bunter, and with a man on first you always have to guard against the bunt. McAndrews looks to your catcher for the sign, shakes a couple off, then gets one he likes. He brings his hands to his belt. The runner takes his lead, and there's a quick throw to first . . . not in time! Close play. Malley had a big lead and you almost caught him leaning the wrong way.

McAndrews is set again. He glances to first. Up comes the leg, around comes the arm, your third baseman's charging, here's the pitch . . . it's bunted toward third and the third baseman, Chris Freeman, fields it cleanly. He's trying for the man at second, here's the long throw . . . it's . . . not in time, everyone's safe!

My hunch was right, but Malley was just too quick for us. We took a chance and went for the lead runner, and Freeman played it perfectly, but Malley was just too fast. Now there are good runners on first and second, and no one out.

My gut tells me they'll try a double steal. I know most managers wouldn't pitch out in this situation, because it wastes a ball and we risk loading the bases, but I feel certain they'll be running with the pitch.

▲ *To pitch out, turn to page 40*

▲ *If you don't want to pitch out, turn to page 42*

19

*H*ere comes the home plate umpire to break up the meeting at the mound. The manager tips his cap at the ump and trots back to the dugout. The Protons have their leadoff man, Malley, on first and an excellent bunter, centerfielder Carlos Ferrer, at the plate. Ferrer is batting .305, with seven home runs and 48 RBIs.

McAndrews looks in for the sign from the catcher, makes the one-second stop at the belt as he checks the runner on first. Here's the delivery . . . it's bunted down the third-base line! What a beauty! The third baseman, Chris Freeman, bare-hands it, looks to second, but sees no chance to get the speedy runner. Now he fires to first . . . in time. The sacrifice is successful. Ferrer continues to dazzle us with his bunting skill.

Now there's one out and a man on second, which brings up their rookie third baseman, Sam Alexander. He's having a solid first year, batting .268, with 10 homers and 34 RBIs. The pitcher's into the stretch, here's the delivery . . . it's swung on and grounded to the right side. Your second baseman takes it on an easy hop from second and throws to first, two away. Malley makes it to third on the play.

That brings up their slumping rightfielder, Luis Acosta. He takes the first pitch for a strike, fouls off the next two, and swings and misses at strike three. Looks like he's still in his slump as he strands the runner at third and ends the inning.

You're up. Leading off is your speedy centerfielder, Rob Burns. Batting .310, with two home runs and 44 RBIs, this guy's a tremendous runner with 38 stolen bases. The first pitch by their big righthander, Wilson, is way inside . . . it hits him! What a way to open the bottom half of the inning. Burns is glaring out at the mound. There's no love lost between these two clubs, but you have to believe that nobody wants to put a speedy leadoff man on base in the bottom of the first.

That brings up your rightfielder, Guy Diego, a strong contender for Rookie of the Year, with his .280 batting average, 14 home runs, and 51 RBIs.

Here's the pitch, there goes Burns and . . . it's a fly ball to left—easy play, one away. Burns retreats to first. That brings up your third baseman, Chris Freeman. He's got good power, with 20 home runs and 77 ribbies. He takes a called strike three, and now there are two outs.

My cleanup hitter's up next. Berico leads the team in home runs with 30 and RBIs with 91, but he's been struggling with his average, which now stands at .247. This would be a perfect time for Berico to break out of his slump. In fact, something tells me he's going to get a hit. I've got my best runner on first. I'm going to flash a sign to my third-base coach before the pitch. I think I should have Burns try for third on a base hit. But then if he's thrown out, that's the inning, and I waste the hot hitter coming up next.

▲ *To have the runner try for third, turn to page 44*

▲ *To have the runner stop at second, turn to page 46*

21

With Burns on first, that brings up your rookie rightfielder, Guy Diego. A strong candidate for Rookie of the Year honors, this kid's having a good all-around season. He's batting .280, with 14 home runs, 51 RBIs, and 15 stolen bases. Wilson goes into his motion, checks the runner, here's the pitch—and there goes Burns! He got a good jump, here's the throw, the slide . . . safe! Stolen base number 39 for Rob Burns.

Diego is still up. He hits the next pitch toward the hole at short . . . it's through for a base hit. Here comes Burns around third, trying to score. The throw comes in, but it's not in time. Burns scores, but the cut-off man holds Diego at first. You take the lead, 1-0.

Your third baseman, Chris Freeman, is up with a man on first, nobody out. He hits a ground ball to short—this could be a two. The shortstop throws to second for one, the ball is relayed to first—double play! With two outs and nobody on, your cleanup hitter, Al Beirco, steps to the plate. He's got 30 home runs and 91 RBIs, but he's been slumping lately. He pops up to end the inning.

There's no score in the second and no score in the third. In the top of the fourth inning, their catcher, Nick Klein ties the game—with a home run to right. You fail to score in your half of the fourth.

In the top of the fifth the Protons pitcher Zeke Wilson starts off the inning with a strikeout. That brings up their leadoff hitter, the second baseman, Steve Malley. The pitcher, Torres, delivers, and it's smacked to center. Robbie Burns charges . . . he won't get it. It drops in for a base hit. Burns plays it on a short hop and tosses the ball to second.

That'll bring up their centerfielder, Carlos Ferrer. So far, he has reached base on a fielder's choice and flied out. Here's the pitch . . . it's lined up the alley in right. This will be extra bases. Your rightfielder, Diego, bobbles the ball. Here comes the runner—Malley scores all the way from first. Ferrer is trying for third, and the throw is . . . not in time. A triple and an RBI, and the Protons take the lead 2-1!

We sure better hold it right there. I don't want Ferrer to come in from third. He's got good speed, though. He's stolen 11 bases this year. Would they try to squeeze him home this early in the game by having the hitter bunt as Ferrer breaks for home? They've got the lead, that's a pretty good time to squeeze.

The next guy is that rookie, Alexander. He whiffed his first time up, but he's a really good fastball hitter. He could do some damage. I'd like to bring my infield in to cut off this extra run, but if I do and he connects, I'm raising this kid's batting average by 40 points, making him a .300 hitter, which he's not.

▲ *To keep the infield at normal depth, turn to page 48*

▲ *To bring the infield in, turn to page 50*

With the leadoff man safely on, that brings up your No. 2 hitter, Guy Diego, the rookie rightfielder. He's batting .280 and has decent power, with 14 homers and 51 RBIs. The infield's back at double-play depth at shortstop and second base, but they're looking for a bunt at first and third. Here's the pitch. Diego turns and bunts it toward first. The first baseman charges, makes the bare-handed pickup, he's trying for Burns at second, here's the slide, the tag, he's . . . out at second! The Protons got the lead runner.

With one away and a man on first, your third baseman, Chris Freeman, stands in. Freeman has had another solid year, batting .267, with 20 homers and 77 RBIs. Once again the pitcher comes to the belt, checks the runner, now the pitch . . . it's swung on and hit sharply toward first. Oh, nice stab by the first baseman! He's got the ball and throws to second for one out. Here comes the return throw to the pitcher covering first . . . got the runner by a step. That was a close one at first, but it's a double play to end the inning. Here comes the manager. He's face to face with the first-base umpire.

Are you nuts? He beat that by a full step. What do you mean, it wasn't even close? Hey, do I ever argue if I'm wrong? O.K., O.K., I'm shutting up, I'm sitting down. But he was safe.

*I*t's now the top of the sixth inning of a scoreless pitching duel between two of the league's best righthanders. The Protons rightfielder makes the first out of the inning, flying out to deep leftfield. That brings up their first baseman, John Neff. He's having a terrific year, batting .280, with 28 home runs and 89 RBIs, and he has been on a tear for the last 15 games, batting .409.

Bombo Torres works around him and runs the count to three balls and one strike. Torres is into his motion, now the pitch . . . check swing. Did he hold up in time? The catcher, Gonzalez, looks to the first base umpire . . . yes, he held in time, ball four. Neff walks. Torres walks the next batter too. Gonzalez trots out to the mound for a quick talk with Torres and gives him a pat on the behind.

The Protons catcher, Nick Klein, is up now. Not a bad hitter—he's got 11 home runs and has driven in 49 runs. He's hitting .261. With men at first and second on two consecutive walks, Bombo might be getting tired. There's warm-up activity in the bullpen.

Bombo continues to be wild and walks the third batter in a row! He's really having trouble finding the strike zone, and his worried manager trots out to the mound.

What's going on here? How do you feel? You sure you're O.K.? I've had Freddie Dunn, the sinkerball reliever, loosening up in the pen, just in case. What I really need now is a double play, and when I need two out, I usually go to Freddie, hoping to get a ground ball. Is your arm getting tired? You sure? Their Number 8 hitter, Walker Smith, is coming up, followed by the pitcher, Wilson, so it shouldn't be too hard to work out of this inning.

▲ *To bring in your sinkerball reliever, turn to page 51*

▲ *To stay with your starter, turn to page 52*

M

en are at first and third, with no one out. That brings up the Protons rookie third baseman, Sam Alexander. He's batting .268, with 10 home runs and 34 RBIs. The infield's at double-play depth and the outfield's straight away on this pull hitter.

Your pitcher, Torres, is ready now. He comes to the set position, checks the runners, now the pitch . . . it's a line drive pulled down the leftfield line that looks like extra bases! One run scores. The runner from first, Ferrer, pulls in at third standing up, and Alexander stops at second with a double.

The Protons lead, 1-0. That starts warm-up action in the bullpen and brings up the Protons' rightfielder, Luis Acosta, who's in a slump but who still leads the league in home runs with 39. Men are on second and third, nobody out. Even though Acosta's been disappointing lately, he's always dangerous. Torres is too careful about giving up a hit, and walks Acosta to load the bases for the hottest hitter on their team, John Neff. Neff, the first-baseman, is batting .280, with 28 homers and 89 RBIs, but he's been hitting close to .400 over his last 15 games. Well, this is quite a bind. Bases loaded, no outs, and the Protons' hottest hitter is up.

Torres will work from a full windup. Now the pitch . . . it's swung on and hit deep to right. Your rightfielder, Guy Diego, is going back, back—he leaps up and . . . the ball hits off the top of the wall! It's rolling into the corner. One run scores, two runs score, and Neff is digging for third as the third run scores. Diego finally gets to the ball and throws it back in, but not before a bases-clearing triple puts the Protons up 4-0. That missed being a grand slam by inches, and the manager has got to be concerned about his pitcher's performance.

hat rookie third baseman should never have gotten on base. In the minors, they always put an outfield shift on him, but obviously he's learned to hit the other way; he puts just enough doubt in the minds of managers like me to create situations like this. I have to believe that had the shift been on, my leftfielder would have had a chance at catching that one.

Then the walk, that was bad enough. But how could my pitcher give up a bases-clearing triple? He looks like he's had it. I've got my lefty ace, Ron Murphy, warming up. I usually like to use him in a save situation, and this is anything but that. Still, my other lefties are either injured or burned out from all the extra-inning games we've played lately. I don't know—I might be better off letting my starter work his way out of it, hope we can come back, and then bring in my ace when we're a bit closer.

▲ *If you leave your starter in, turn to page 32*

▲ *If you bring in your ace reliever, turn to page 36*

29

With runners at first and third and nobody out, the Protons' rookie third baseman, Sam Alexander, steps up to the plate. He's having a good first season, batting .268, with 10 home runs and 34 RBIs. Your infield is at double-play depth, the outfield's shifted around toward left, expecting the batter to pull. Your pitcher comes to the stop. He checks the two runners, now the pitch . . . it's a line drive to left field, your left-fielder is charging and he . . . makes the catch. The runner from third, Ferrer, heads for home. Here comes the throw . . . not in time. A sacrifice fly and an RBI, and the Protons lead 1-0. That particular hunch paid off. If the shift hadn't been on, there is no way the leftfielder would have gotten to that ball in time. The rookie has still not perfected going the other way. The next batter strikes out, followed by a pop-up, and the inning is over.

In the fourth the Protons pick up another run on a solo shot by their first baseman, John Neff, whose hot streak continues. That's his 29th homer of the year, and you trail 2-0, even though your pitcher is not pitching badly at all.

The batters are retired in order in the fifth and sixth. You go to the bottom of the seventh, still trailing, 2-0. Your first baseman, Judd Jackson, leads off with a base hit, but your shortstop strikes out and your catcher flies out, bringing up Torres, your pitcher.

reat. We're down by two in the seventh inning and my pitcher's up. If we had a guy in scoring position I'd pinch hit for him for sure. But now, with a runner on first? And two outs? Torres is not a great-hitting pitcher, but he has gotten a few clutch hits for us this year.

I have a good pinch hitter on the bench, but I'd like to save him for a situation that could put us ahead, or at least tie it up. Besides, Torres has been pitching well—his only mistakes were giving up a sacrifice fly and making one bad pitch to the hottest hitter in the world. I have a hunch he can finish out this game if I leave him in.

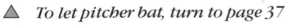 *To let pitcher bat, turn to page 37*

▲ *To pinch hit, turn to page 38*

31

You've decided to leave your starter in. You feel that Torres can settle down and at least finish out the inning. That'll bring up the Protons leftfielder, Trevor Nelson. He's batting .240, with 14 home runs and 50 RBIs. With a man on third and no one out, the infield plays in. Here's the pitch ... fly ball to straightaway center, not very deep. Neff moves back to third. But wait a minute—with a four-run lead, he tags up and plans to head home! The centerfielder makes the catch and there goes Neff. The throw is coming to the plate; it's going to be close. Here's the slide, the tag, he's ... *out* at the plate, double play! The Protons took a chance and sent Neff, and now there are two away. Next up is their catcher, Nick Klein, who takes a called strike three. After a disastrous start to the inning, Torres comes back and gets three quick outs.

Your centerfielder, Rob Burns, leads off, lines the first pitch into right center, and coasts into second with a double. That brings up your rookie rightfielder, Guy Diego, who's hitting .280, with 14 home runs and 51 RBIs. Diego grounds the ball over the first-base bag. It's rolling into rightfield and here comes Burns ... he'll score. Diego is on his way to second, and the throw is not in time. Back-to-back doubles, and your offense has come out roaring here in the bottom of the first inning! You now trail 4-1, with a man on second and nobody out.

Here comes your third baseman, Chris Freeman. An all-round solid player, Freeman is batting .267, with 20 homers and 77 RBIs. Freeman hits a ground ball to the

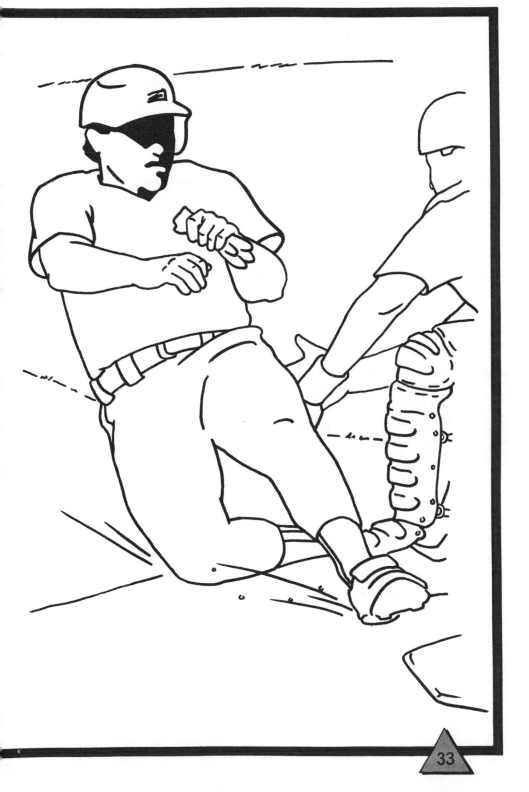

33

right side. This will move the runner to third. The second baseman throws to first—one away.

Here comes your cleanup hitter, Al Berico, a guy with good power, who's hit 30 home runs and has 91 RBIs. He struggling a bit with his average, which has slipped to .247. He hits a fly ball to fairly deep center—this should score the run. Their centerfielder makes the catch, Freeman tags and . . . scores easily. It's now a 4-2 ball game, with two outs. Your second baseman, Patrick Berry, pops it up to shortstop to end the inning, but you are able to get back two runs.

Your starter, Torres, settles into a groove and retires 20 out of the next 21 batters, including 14 in a row. The Protons starter, Zeke Wilson, settles in as well, and you go to the bottom of the eighth still down 4-2. With one out, your centerfielder, Burns, launches a drive deep to left. This one is way back and . . . it's out of here! It's a solo shot, only his third homer of the year, but oh what a timely one. The Protons lead is cut to 4-3. Your right-fielder ends the inning with a strikeout. The Protons fail to score in the top of the ninth, so your team bats in the bottom of the ninth, down by a run.

Your third baseman, Freeman, leads off the ninth with a walk. Then Berico flies out, but Freeman doesn't advance. Berry then lines a hard single to left, which gets there too quickly for Freeman to get to third from first. So you have men on first and second, one away, with your first baseman, Judd Jackson, up. He's a solid .271 hitter, and he's driven in 54 runs this year.

e've got the tying run at second, with one out and a good hitter at the plate. I'd like to send the runners with the pitch, first to keep out of the double play, and also because if Judd gets a hit, we have a chance of getting the winning run around from first. But if I sent them and Judd doesn't make contact, the lead runner, Freeman, could be thrown out, which would take the winning run off the bases and make it two outs. My instincts say run, but it could cost us the game.

▲ To send the runners with the pitch, turn to page 53

▲ To not send the runners, turn to page 54

35

*T*hat'll be all for your starter. He got hit very hard and he's being taken out right here. The new pitcher you've brought in is a lefty, the ace of your bullpen. He's had a tremendous year, with a record of 6-1, 21 saves, 88 strikeouts, and only 40 walks in 94 innings of work. His 1.96 ERA is second in the league.

You want to stop this rally right now. The pitcher will be facing their leftfielder, who's batting .240 with 14 home runs and 50 RBIs. Your lefty reliever's first pitch is lined over the shortstop's head . . . base hit. In comes the man from third, and it's a 5-0 ball game. Your reliever works his way out of the inning with a strike-out, a fly-ball out and another strikeout, but you trail 5-0.

Your bullpen holds them for the rest of the game. You score a run in the third on a double by your center-fielder and a single by your third baseman, a run in the seventh on a solo homer by your catcher, and a run in the ninth on a walk to your first baseman, a stolen base, and an RBI single by your shortstop. But you can't come all the way back, and you go on to lose, 5-3.

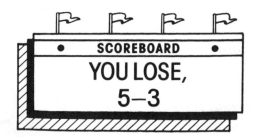

SCOREBOARD

YOU LOSE,
5–3

36

*I*t looks like Torres will bat here in the seventh. There's a man on first, two away. Torres looks at two strikes and then swings and lines a base hit over second! The lead runner, Jackson, is on his way to third . . . he'll make it standing up.

That brings up centerfielder Rob Burns. Here's the pitch . . . he hits a slow tapper past the mound. The shortstop makes a bare-handed pickup, now the throw to first . . . *safe*, and the run scores! Your rightfielder flies out to end the inning. Torres stays in the game and doesn't allow anyone to reach base. You bat in the bottom of the ninth, trailing 2-1.

Your first baseman, Judd Jackson, leads off the inning with a walk. The next batter, the shortstop, John Miner delivers a double, scoring Jackson all the way from first because he was running with the pitch. You've tied the game at 2-2.

That brings up your catcher, Pedro Gonzalez. They bring in their stopper, Snipe Conley, who hits a ground ball through the gap between first and second for a base hit. Miner rounds third! Here comes the throw to the plate from the rightfielder. Here's the slide, he is . . . safe! You win, 3-2, and move into postseason play!

SCOREBOARD

YOU WIN,
3—2!

A change has been made. We're going to get a pinch hitter for the pitcher, Torres. Bombo has pitched well, but he does trail 2-0, and is being lifted in an attempt to generate some runs here in the seventh with two out and one man on. The righty pinch hitter, Ben Mooney, steps up to the plate. He's batting .308 as a pinch hitter, the best in the league. He's also hit four home runs and driven in 17 runs, and has good speed on the basepaths.

The Protons pitcher, Wilson, looks in for the sign, comes to the set position, then stops at the belt, checking Jackson, the man on first. Here's the delivery . . . it's swung on and hit deep to left, this one looks good enough; if it stays fair, it's gone, it is . . . *out* of here! Mooney delivers a game-tying, two-run, pinch-hit home run! The fans are on their feet, shouting for a curtain call. Mooney comes to the top step of the dugout and tips his cap. Another cheer goes up. We've got a brand-new ball game!

Your next batter strikes out to end the inning. You bring in your lefty ace, Ron Murphy, with his 1.96 ERA, and he shuts down the Protons in the eighth and ninth innings.

You go to the bottom of the ninth with the game still tied, 2-2.

Your first baseman, Judd Jackson, leads off with a walk, steals second and crosses to third on a groundout by your shortstop. Your catcher, Pedro Gonzalez, steps up to the plate with one out and a man on third. You're in perfect position to win this game right here. The Protons play their infield in to try to cut off the winning run at the plate. Their outfield is shallow, only as deep as they can throw, because anything hit farther would make it impossible to throw out Jackson tagging from third.

Their pitcher's ready. Gonzalez settles into the batter's box, here's the pitch . . . he hits a fly ball to center. The centerfielder looks up, starts to run after the ball but then stops. It's over his head! That'll be the ballgame! The run scores and you win, 3-2. Score it a single and an RBI for Gonzalez! With this victory, you win the division and head for the playoffs!

SCOREBOARD

YOU WIN,
3–2!

There are men at first and second, nobody out. That brings up the Protons rookie third baseman, Sam Alexander. This youngster's batting .268, with 10 home runs and 34 RBIs. McAndrews is into his motion, the runners take their leads, now here's the pitch . . . and the runners are going. But it's a pitchout! The catcher fires to third . . . gets him! You anticipated the double steal and cut down the lead runner. That leaves a man on second with one out.

McAndrews walks the next batter. That brings up their cleanup hitter, Luis Acosta. This kid leads the league in home runs with 39, but he's been in a slump for the last 10 games. The runner on second takes his lead, here's the pitch . . . it's a line drive, caught by your second baseman, Patrick Berry, who steps on the bag to double up the runner. An unassisted double play ends the inning.

The game remains scoreless until the sixth. Your rookie rightfielder, Guy Diego, bats in the bottom of the sixth with two men out and hits a towering drive to left center. The leftfielder goes to the wall, he times his leap, his glove goes up over the wall . . . but the ball is gone! Just inches over the glove of the leaping leftfielder! You take the lead 1-0 on this solo blast, Diego's fifteenth home run of the year. The next batter, third baseman Chris Freeman, flys out to center for the final out of the inning.

In the top of the eighth, your lead remains 1-0. The Protons open the inning with back-to-back singles by their first baseman and leftfielder. You strike out their catcher. It's first and third, with one away. Their short-stop, Walker Smith, is up next.

Men at first and third, one out. We've got a one-run lead and it's looking pretty slim. I guess they don't come any slimmer than this. I want to keep the man on third from scoring, so I'd like to bring my infield in to cut off the run at the plate. But by bringing my infield in, I take this .256-hitting shortstop and turn him into a .300 hitter, which he most definitely is not. He could line one over my shortstop's head.

I could set up for the double play, figuring that would get me out of the inning and strand the guy at third. But then if they beat out the front end of the double play, the guy from third would score on the force-out. I'd hate to give up the tying run on an out. I'd really hate that.

▲ *To bring the infield in, turn to page 56*

▲ *To set the infield at double play depth, turn to page 58*

41

We've got men at first and second, nobody out. That brings up their rookie third baseman, Sam Alexander, who's batting .268, with 10 home runs and 34 RBIs. McAndrews is into his motion, the runners take their leads, now here's the pitch. The runners go, and the throw to third to nail the lead runner is . . . not in time. It's a successful double steal, leaving men on second and third with nobody out. That brings up the league's leading home-run hitter, rightfielder, Luis Acosta. He's batting .260, with those 39 homers and 106 RBIs.

This is a fine jam to be in this early in the game. Do I issue an intentional walk to Acosta to set up the double play, and be satisfied with getting out of the inning only one run down? This guy leads the league in home runs, and he's got over 100 RBIs. It makes sense to walk him.

But the guy behind him in the order, their first baseman, John Neff, is also a good home run hitter. He's hit 28 this year, and he's been on a hot streak for the last 15 games, hitting close to .400, while Acosta has been in a slump.

Do I pitch to the slumping hitter who leads the league in homers, or do I load the bases for the hot hitter so I have a shot at the double play?

▲ *To pitch to the rightfielder, turn to page 60*

▲ *To walk the rightfielder, turn to page 61*

43

Rob Burns is rounding second on the base hit. He's on his way to third, the throw from their right-fielder is a strong peg, they may get him. Here's the slide, the tag . . . he's *out* at third! It was a gutsy play, try-ing to advance the runner, but the inning ends with no score.

Several scoreless innings go by. In the bottom of the fourth Burns leads off with a double. After Diego strikes out, Freeman smacks another double to give you a 1-0 lead. Your leftfielder, Al Berico, who's been struggling, flies out for the second out of the inning and then Patrick Berry singles home the man on second. Your first baseman, Judd Jackson, flies out to end the inning, but you've grabbed a 2-0 lead.

In the top of the sixth the Protons leadoff man, Steve Malley, walks and steals second. Then Carlos Ferrer beats out a bunt. Now there are men at first and third, no outs. Then you surrender a crushing three-run homer to the league's hottest hitter, John Neff, his 29th home run of the year. The Protons go ahead 3-2 before the inning ends on a fly-out.

In the bottom of the sixth, Burns singles. Following a pop-out by Diego, Chris Freeman triples, scoring Burns from first and tying the game. Al Berico then strikes out, but Patrick Berry comes through with a clutch single and you regain the lead, 4-3. Judd Jackson flies out again to end the inning.

In the top of the seventh their catcher, Nick Klein, leads off with a walk. Shortstop Walker Smith sacrifices him over to second, and Klein scores on a rare base hit by their pitcher. They've tied the game at 4-4 with one out. The leadoff man, Malley, sacrifices the pitcher over to second. He then scores on a clutch hit by Carlos Ferrer to take the lead back. Their third baseman grounds out to second to end the inning. They have gained the lead, 5-4.

Now it's the bottom of the seventh. Your shortstop, John Miner, just up from Triple A and batting only .231, gets a leadoff walk. Your catcher, Pedro Gonzalez, gets a base hit, and there are runners at first and second, no outs. Your pitcher is up in an obvious bunting situation, but he bunts the first two pitches foul for an 0-and-2 count.

This goes back to spring training. Work on your bunting, I'd say. At morning practice and at afternoon practice. Bunting is the best way for pitchers to contribute offensively. I tell them that I don't care if they don't get a single base hit all year. As long as they sacrifice the man over, they're doing their job!

Now I've got two strikes on a pitcher who strikes out a lot and has hit into a bunch of double plays this year. Do I have him bunt again and risk the easy strikeout if he can't lay it down? Or do I let him swing away? At least that way the ball could be put into play. Of course, it could be put into play for an easy two outs!

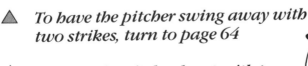 ▲ *To have the pitcher swing away with two strikes, turn to page 64*

▲ *To have the pitcher bunt with two strikes, turn to page 65*

T he runner, Burns, holds at second on Berico's base hit, giving you men on first and second, with two men out. That brings up your second baseman, Patrick Berry, a great defensive player who's having a decent year at the plate, batting .255, with 12 home runs and 60 RBIs. He's a good clutch hitter, too.

Their pitcher is into his motion. He checks the runners, now the pitch ... it's swung on, hit deep to left, this one is way back—going, going, kiss it good-bye! A three-run home run for Berry, his 13th of the year, and you jump out to a 3-0 lead. Next up is your first baseman, Judd Jackson, who flies out to right to end the inning.

Both pitchers settle down and the game moves along to the top of the seventh. Their red-hot first baseman, John Neff, leads off and lines a base hit back up the middle. That brings up their leftfielder, Trevor Nelson, who lays down a beautiful sacrifice bunt, moving the runner to second. Their catcher, Nick Klein, comes through with an RBI base hit to get them on the board finally, and it's a 3-1 game, with one out and a man on first. Their shortstop, Walker Smith, draws a walk, bringing up their pitcher in a first-and-second situation. They leave him in and he executes their second successful sacrifice of the inning to move the runners up to second and third, with two away.

That brings up their leadoff batter, the speedy second baseman, Steve Malley. He hits a line shot to left for a base hit. One run will score, and they're sending in the man from second. This'll be close, here's the throw, he's

46

... out at the plate! The inning is over, but they score two and cut your lead to 3-2.

In the top of the ninth, two base hits and a walk load the bases for the Protons with no one out.

McAndrews has been pitching well all game, but I have to find out if he's O.K. Everybody! I want the whole infield here. You feel all right, Mac? Yeah? O.K., I'm going to leave you in to handle this. You look like your stuff is still pretty sharp. The two pitches they hit this inning were good ones. They just guessed right on you, that's all.

The question is, do we play the infield in to cut off the tying run? Their next batter is the shortstop, Walker Smith. He's hitting .256, but he has driven in 40 runs. Pretty good for a Number 8 hitter. If we pull you guys in to the edge of the grass, we raise his average 40 points. We could also play second and short at double-play depth—about halfway between the infield and outfield grass—and guard the lines at first and third to prevent the extra-base hit that could give them the lead. But that way, even an infield out will tie the game. Here comes the ump, this meeting is over.

▲ *To guard the lines and go to double play depth, turn to page 66*

▲ *To bring the infield in, turn to page 68*

47

With one out and a man on third, the Protons rookie third baseman, Sam Alexander, comes to the plate. He's batting .268, with 10 home runs and 34 RBIs. The infield is back at normal depth. Torres, the pitcher, works from a full windup. Here's the pitch . . . ground ball deep in the hole at short! The shortstop, Miner, backhands the ball but his only play is at first. The throw is in time, but the run scores. You trail 3-1 with two away in the fifth inning. That brings up the Protons right-fielder, Luis Acosta, who strikes out to end the inning.

No one scores in the sixth, seventh or eighth. Your team is up in the bottom of the ninth, still trailing 3-1. Your catcher, Pedro Gonzalez, leads off with a base hit up the middle. With the pitcher scheduled to bat, you decide to send up your lefty pinch hitter, Brent Moore. However Moore lofts a lazy fly ball to right for the first out. Your leadoff man, centerfielder Rob Burns, is up next, and he lines a base hit to right. You have men at first and second, one out.

Guy Diego, the rightfielder, steps up and hits a ground ball to the right side of the infield. The Protons second baseman's only play is to first. Your runners advance to second and third, putting the tying run into scoring position, but now there are two outs. It's all up to your third baseman, Chris Freeman. Freeman's a solid ballplayer with a respectable 77 RBIs this year. He has a knack for coming through in the clutch.

Zeke Wilson gets his sign from the catcher. He'll work from the full windup. Here's the pitch . . . it's swung on and hit deep to right! It's way back—this one could be out of here! The rightfielder, Acosta, runs back to the wall, leaps and ... *makes the catch!* What a play! That ball was up above the wall! Acosta took a home run—what would have been a game-winning home run—away from Freeman. Instead, you lose, 3-1, on a heart-stopping play. The fans shuffle silently out of the stadium, unable to believe what they just saw.

With one away and a man on third, you bring the infield in to try to cut the run off at the plate. Bombo Torres, the pitcher, will work from a full windup, against their rookie rightfielder, Acosta. Torres is into his motion, now the pitch . . . it's a hard-hit grounder to the shortstop. Ferrer, the man on third, is trying to score. The shortstop throws home. Here's the play at the plate, Ferrer is . . . out at home! A sharp throw by John Miner, the shortstop, nails the runner at home. Two outs. That brings up their third baseman, Sam Alexander, who strikes out to end the inning.

No one scores in the sixth, seventh or eighth. You come up in the bottom of the ninth, still trailing 2-1. Your catcher, Pedro Gonzalez, leads off the ninth with a base hit. Going against the percentages, you pinch hit for your pitcher with your righty pinch hitter, Ben Mooney, the league's best this year. Gonzalez takes his lead off first. Wilson comes to the one-second stop, now the delivery . . . the ball is hit high and deep to left centerfield. The leftfielder is looking up, and that ball is *out* of here! A two-run, game-winning blast in the bottom of the ninth by Mooney, the pinch hitter. You win the game 3-2, and the division.

*T*hat's going to be it for the starter. The sinkerball specialist, Freddie Dunn, will be coming into a bases-loaded, one-out situation. The manager's strategy must be to try to get the next batter to hit into a double play. The sinkerball, of course, is more likely to be hit on the ground than any other pitch, so that's what we'll be looking for here.

Dunn has completed his warm-ups. The shortstop, Walker Smith, steps up to the plate. Dunn has his sign, he'll work from the stretch as usual, now here's the pitch . . . it's in the dirt, it gets away from the catcher! Here comes the runner from third with the first run of the game.

Oh, talk about a plan backfiring. In comes the sinkerball pitcher to try for the ground ball, but instead the pitch drops too far, hits the dirt and scoots away from the catcher. You trail 1-0.

There is no further scoring, and you go on to lose a heartbreaker, 1-0.

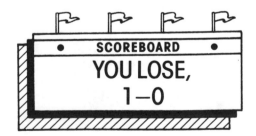

SCOREBOARD

YOU LOSE,
1−0

*S*o, you're sticking with the starter, Bombo Torres. We'll see if he can work out of his own jam. The Protons shortstop, Walker Smith, steps up to the plate. Here's the pitch . . . it's popped up to the right side for an easy out. The hard-throwing righthander gets the big out he needed without giving up a run. Now let's see if he can get out of the inning.

Their pitcher, Zeke Wilson, steps up to bat. I guess they figure they need his pitching and will get another scoring opportunity. They better—Wilson takes a called third strike to end the sixth.

The game remains a scoreless pitchers' duel until the eighth. With two outs and nobody on base in the bottom of the inning, your pitcher, Torres, bats. He's hitting .138 this year but he has gotten several clutch RBIs. Here's the pitch . . . it's hit well, deep to left. This could go all the way! It's . . . out of here! Torres hits his first major-league home run, and it couldn't have come at a better time! They're mobbing him in the dugout!

Your pitcher, riding high after his home run, retires the Protons in order in the top of the ninth to pick up the win, 1-0, and a spot in the playoffs. You can't have a better game than he had today!

SCOREBOARD

YOU WIN,
1−0!

It's the bottom of the ninth, men on first and second, with one away. Judd Jackson is at the plate. The pitcher, Wilson, is ready, here's the stretch . . . he throws to first, not in time. The man on first, Berry, had a pretty good lead that time, so Wilson threw over there to keep him honest. Now we're ready, Wilson throws . . . the runners are going with the pitch. It's swung on and *drilled* into the gap in left center. This will be extra bases. The runner on second, Freeman, scores to tie it up.

The ball is bouncing near the warning track, and their leftfielder, Trevor Nelson, can't get a handle on it. Here comes Berry around third. He's trying to score! Nelson, in leftfield, finally gets the ball and fires to the cutoff man at short, who turns and throws to the plate. Here's the slide, the tag . . . he's safe! You sent the runners with the pitch, and Berry scored all the way from first, giving you the winning run. You win 5-4 and take the division!

SCOREBOARD

YOU WIN,
5—4!

Judd Jackson, your first baseman, steps up to the plate with men at first and second, one out in the bottom of the ninth. The runners take their leads. Zeke Wilson is into his stretch, the one-second stop, now the delivery . . . the runners aren't going. The pitch is swung on and drilled into the gap in left center, this'll fall in for extra bases. One run will score to tie it up, 4-4. Their leftfielder, Trevor Nelson, plays it off the wall and throws to the cutoff man, who turns and holds the runner, Berry, on third as Jackson pulls in with a stand-up double.

It's now a tie game, men at second and third with one out. That will bring up your shortstop, John Miner. Here's the pitch. Miner hits a fly ball fairly shallow in right. It's curving foul, but it looks like their rightfielder, Luis Acosta, will have a shot at it in foul territory. He's over near the stands, he . . . makes the catch with his back toward home plate. What's going to happen to Berry, the lead runner?

*T*he ball is caught, now my job begins. Should I signal Berry to try to tag up? The ball wasn't hit very deep, but Acosta caught it anyway. I think Berry may be able to score from third with the winning run. There's a lot at stake, but we have a chance to take it all here.

▲ *To have the runner tag up, turn to page 69*

▲ *To have the runner hold on third, turn to page 70*

55

*T*hey have runners on first and third and one away, here in the top of the eighth. The shortstop, Walker Smith, is up. You bring your infield in to try and keep the man on third from coming home and tying the game. McAndrews is into his stretch, he checks the runners, around comes the arm . . . it's a sharply hit ground ball that's bouncing just past your third baseman Chris Freeman's glove. The man on third scores. The man on first stops at second, but the damage has been done. Because the infield was in, that sharply hit ball was easily a hit. Had Freeman been playing back, he probably could have grabbed it and stopped the run from scoring, and maybe even gotten an inning-ending double play. Instead, we're all tied in the eighth, 1-1.

Because the game is tied, their pitcher, Zeke Wilson, who's been doing a very good job, will bat for himself. There are men at first and second, one out. Here's the pitch . . . it's hit on the ground toward second, this could be a double play. The second baseman throws to the shortstop, John Miner, who steps on the bag for one, and fires to first . . . in time. You get the double play and the inning is over.

The game stays tied until the bottom of the ninth. Your rookie rightfielder, Guy Diego, leads off the inning with a base hit to right. The winning run is on first base.

All right! Winning run on first! I like this kid, Diego, a lot. I think I've found my rightfielder for the next several years. He's got good speed, too, with 15 stolen bases this year. He's been thrown out more than he should have been, but he'll learn.

I'd really love to send him right now, have him try to steal second so the winning run will be in scoring position. But if he's thrown out, I erase the winning run from the base paths.

We're tied, not losing by a run, so we don't have to score this inning to stay alive. Maybe it's best to play it conservatively and not send him. Keep him safe on the bases and hope we can build a rally that'll bring him around. On the other hand, it would be sweet, really sweet, to win this thing right here and now with a little gamble and a little hustle.

▲ *To have the runner try to steal second, turn to page 71*

▲ *If you don't want to try to steal second, turn to page 72*

57

*T*he Protons have runners at first and third and one away here in the top of the eighth, with their shortstop, Walker Smith, up at bat. You set the infield back at double-play depth, hoping to get two and get out of the inning right here. Your pitcher is into his stretch, he checks the runners, around comes the arm . . . it's a sharply hit ground ball toward third. This could be two. Your third baseman, Chris Freeman, fields it cleanly, whips it to second for one, around to first . . . double play! An around-the-horn double play, third to second to first, and you get out of a sticky situation without allowing a run.

You fail to score in the bottom of the eighth. In the top of the ninth, their centerfielder, not known for his power, hits a surprise home run and ties the game at 1-1.

You're up in the bottom of the ninth. Your leftfielder, Al Berico, leads off the inning with a base-on ball. That brings up your second baseman, Patrick Berry, who lays down a bunt. It's a beauty, fielded by their pitcher, Wilson. His only play is to first, and the sacrifice is successful. That gives you a man on second with one away.

After your first baseman lines out to third, your shortstop, John Miner, just called up from Triple A, steps up to the plate. Wilson goes into his stretch. Here's the pitch, and there goes the runner! Berico is trying to steal second. The pitch is swung on and missed, and the throw down to third is . . . not in time! Stolen base. Without the benefit of a base hit, you have a man on third, two out. That brings up your catcher, Pedro Gonzalez.

They pull their infield in and play their outfield shallow because a long fly ball will win the game anyway.

Now Wilson is ready. He's into his full windup, here's the delivery ... high and outside—it gets away from their catcher! It's rolling all the way to the backstop. Here comes Berico in from third with the winning run! They're scoring it a wild pitch. You score the winning run with a walk, sacrifice, stolen base and a wild pitch. You bring the winning run around and take the game, 2-1, and the division.

*H*ere in the first inning, the Protons have men at second and third, nobody out. Here comes Luis Acosta, who is leading the league in home runs with 39. You might walk him intentionally here, or pitch around him, except that next up will be their first baseman, John Neff, who also has good power and is currently the hottest hitter in the league.

It looks like you're going to pitch to Acosta. McAndrews works from the full windup. Here's the pitch . . . it's swung on and clubbed deep to left, going way back. He hit this one a ton! There's no question about this— it's out of here! And a nice catch by a fan in the upper deck. A monster three-run homer and they grab a 3-0 lead.

They score three more runs in the first inning. You never recover and go on to lose, 8-2.

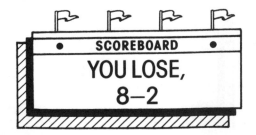

SCOREBOARD

**YOU LOSE,
8—2**

The Protons have got runners at second and third, nobody out, and the league's leading homerun hitter, Luis Acosta, is stepping in. You decide to walk Acosta intentionally, thereby loading the bases and bringing up their hottest hitter, first baseman John Neff. He's got good power, too, with 28 homers this year. He's also knocked in 89 runs, and right here he has a chance to add to that total. The Protons could break the game open here in the first if their hitters deliver.

Defensively, you have to be thinking of setting up for the double play and the chance for a force at any base. Well, we're set. Neff steps in. McAndrews will work from a full windup. Here's the pitch . . . it's a ground ball hit right to short. This could be the double-play ball you were hoping for. The shortstop, John Miner, fires to second for one. The second baseman, Patrick Berry, makes the pivot, leaping over the sliding runner trying to take him out of the play, and the throw to first is . . . in time, doubleplay! The runner from second crosses to third on the play.

One run scores, but it could have been a lot worse. Credit Neff with an RBI on the play; he now has 90 for the year. But you now have two outs, and only the runner at third to worry about. That brings up their left-fielder, Trevor Nelson, who hits a fly ball to shallow right, an easy play to end the inning. They lead, 1-0, but you've got to feel a litle happy about getting out of a first-inning jam only one run behind.

There's no further scoring through the sixth. In the top of the seventh, they pick up another run on a dou-

ble by their catcher and an RBI single by their shortstop. You trail 2-0 going to the bottom of the ninth.

Your rightfielder, Guy Diego, leads off with a hit. Following a fly-out by your third baseman, your leftfielder, Al Berico, walks. That brings up second baseman Patrick Berry, who hits a drive deep to center. It's way back there, it's ... out of here! Berry's not known for his power, but this was as good a time as any for a surprise! His bottom-of-the-ninth, three-run home run gives you a come-from-behind 3-2 victory and moves you into the postseason play.

Men are on first and second, nobody out. There's an 0-and-2 count on McAndrews following two fouled-off bunt attempts. Let's see if he'll be bunting again with two strikes or swinging away.

Wilson goes into his motion, here's the pitch . . . the pitch is swung on and grounded to second, this could be two. The Protons second baseman flips to the short-stop covering, then he fires the ball to first . . . in time, double play! The man on second, John Miner, moves over to third on the play, but now there are two outs.

This brings up your leadoff batter, centerfielder Rob Burns. The tying run is 90 feet away here in the seventh inning. Wilson will work from the stretch. Miner, on third, takes a big lead. You could be thinking squeeze here. Their pitcher is at the belt, now he—there's a pickoff play at third . . . he's got Miner! The rookie's been mowed down at third to end the inning! I can't tell if he took too long a lead, or he simply wasn't paying close attention to the pitcher. He'll hear about this in the club-house later. That's it for your team in the seventh.

They bring in their stopper and hold you for the rest of the game. You go on to lose, 5-4.

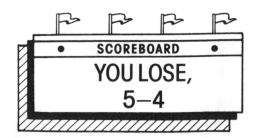

SCOREBOARD

YOU LOSE,
5—4

*T*here are men on first and second, nobody out. The pitcher, McAndrews, faces an 0-and-2 count following two fouled-off bunt attempts. Wilson goes into the stretch, here's the delivery ... it's bunted again, this time it's a beauty. The ball is fielded by their first baseman, whose only play is to first. The sacrifice is successful, a gutsy two-strike bunt laid down perfectly by McAndrews. You now have men at second and third and one away, and Rob Burns is coming to bat with your team trailing 5-4.

*T*he tying run's on third, the go-ahead run is on second. If my batter does get a hit, I'd really like both runs to score, but Gonzalez, on second, has terrible knees. He'd never make it all the way around, even on a sharply hit single. I mean, he's a catcher, what do you expect? I'd really love to pinch-run for him with a speedy guy, but I want Gonzalez's experience and great defensive ability behind the plate in the eighth and ninth.

▲ *To put in a pinch runner for your catcher on second, turn to page 74*

▲ *To leave your catcher in, turn to page 76*

We're in the top of the ninth, bases loaded, nobody out, and you cling to a 3-2 lead. Your pitcher's in a tight jam here. The conference on the mound has ended, and now the Protons shortstop, Walker Smith, steps up to the plate. Your first and third basemen guard the lines against the extra-base hit, while your shortstop and second baseman are back at doubleplay depth, hoping to get two.

McAndrews works from the full windup, and here's the pitch . . . it's a bullet ripped toward the third-base line, snagged on one hop by Chris Freeman at third base, a beautiful off-balance, backhanded pickup. Freeman's only play is to step on the bag at third for the force, and a run scores to tie the game. Freeman made a beautiful play just to get to that ball. The only reason he had a chance was because he was guarding the line. Since he didn't have time to set himself and throw, he did the smart thing and stepped on third for the only out he could get.

Now there's one away, men at first and second, and the game's tied, 3-3. That brings up the pitcher, Wilson, in a bunting situation. He lays down a good one. McAndrews fields it, but his only play is at first. The sacrifice is successful, and now there are two men away, with runners moved up to second and third. Their second baseman pops up to end the inning. You fail to score in the bottom of the ninth, and we go to extra innings with the game tied, 3-3.

No one scores in the 10th or 11th. In the top of the 12th, their leftfielder hits his 15th homer of the year, a solo shot, that puts them ahead, 4-3. You trail in this game for the first time.

In the bottom of the 12th, Rob Burns gets a clutch two-out hit. That brings up your rightfielder, Guy Diego. He works the count to 2 and 1.

I've got my best runner out there. Burns is a kid with great speed who's stolen 38 bases for me this year. I think I should send him with the pitch. With the count at 2 and 1, Wilson has got to come in with something in the strike zone to avoid running up the count and possibly putting the winning run on, so it would be a good pitch on which to play a hit-and-run with Burns running on the pitch to Diego. But if Diego swings and misses, Burns could be thrown out, and that would end the ball game.

▲ *To send the runner on the next pitch, turn to page 84*

▲ *If you don't want to send the runner on the next pitch, turn to page 86*

*T*he conference at the mound is over, the strategy has been decided. The bases are loaded here in the top of the ninth, no outs, and your 3-2 lead seems very much in jeopardy. The Protons shortstop, Walker Smith, will bat. Your infield is playing in, attempting to keep the tying run on third from coming in to score.

McAndrews is ready, he's got his sign. He's working from a full windup, and here's the pitch . . . it's a bullet ripped over the third baseman's head, heading down the line in left. One run is in, here comes the man from second, he'll score, and the batter pulls up at second with a two-RBI double that puts the Protons out in front for the first time today, 4-3. Because your third baseman was playing in, he had no chance to grab that rocket, which bounced near the third-base bag and then skipped down the line into left. The Protons still have men on second and third, with nobody out.

Their pitcher will bat next, now on the plus side of a 4-3 score. He strikes out for the first out of the inning. You walk their centerfielder to load the bases again, and get the double play to end the inning, but you fail to score in the bottom of the ninth, and lose, 4-3, after leading all the way into the ninth.

With only one out here in the bottom of the ninth, your runner on third, Pat Berry, is tagging up, even though the ball was not hit deep. The Protons right-fielder, Luis Acosta, sets himself up in foul territory, makes the catch, and now throws to the plate. Here's the tag. Berry's . . . out at the plate! Well, you took a gamble sending the man, but a good play by Acosta cuts him down at home. The game remains tied, 4-4.

Both teams continue to blow game-winning scoring opportunities in the 10th, 11th and 12th innings. In the bottom of the 13th your third baseman, Chris Freeman, leads off the inning with a solo homer to win the game and the division!

SCOREBOARD

YOU WIN,
5–4!

69

*T*he Protons rightfielder makes the catch in foul ground. Your runner, Pat Berry, tags and takes a few steps down the line toward home to draw the throw. Now the runner scoots back to third. Berry never really intended to tag, he just wanted to force the throw, hoping it would get away from the catcher. But the throw comes in on a perfect line. Had he attempted to tag up he would have been out at home by a mile. It remains second and third, but now there are two men out. It's still a 4-4 tie. That brings up Pedro Gonzales, your catcher.

Their pitcher works from a full windup. Here's the pitch, it's swung on and grounded toward short . . . but it's—booted by their shortstop! In comes Berry from third with the winning run. An error by their shortstop gives you a 5-4 victory and moves you into the playoffs!

SCOREBOARD

YOU WIN,
5–4!

It's the bottom of the ninth, and the game is at 1-1. You have Diego on first, no one out, and making his way to the plate is your third baseman, Chris Freeman. Carefully, Diego measures out his lead once again. The pitcher comes to the stop, looks toward first, now the pitch . . . there he goes, Diego is trying to steal second.

The pitch is high and away. The catcher leaps up and fires down to second. Here comes Diego with a head-first slide, and the ball gets away from their shortstop, who's covering second. Their catcher made a bad throw, and the ball goes into centerfield. Diego gets up and easily makes it to third. You now have the winning run 90 feet away, with nobody out and your cleanup hitter, Al Berico, coming to the plate.

The Protons bring their infield in to try to stop the run and keep the game alive. Their outfield is shallow, only playing as far as they can throw, since a long fly ball would end the game, same as a hit. Your leftfielder, Berico, steps in. Now we're set. Wilson delivers from the full windup . . . it's hit to left, and this could win the ball game. The ball goes over their leftfielder's head and in trots the winning run from third. Score it a single and an RBI. You take the game, 2-1. See you in the playoffs!

SCOREBOARD

YOU WIN,
2–1!

*H*ere in the bottom of the ninth, we're all tied at 1-1. Diego is on first with no one out, and your third baseman, Chris Freeman, coming to the plate. Diego takes his lead, now the pitch . . . it's a base hit going over second. Their centerfielder plays it on the hop and fires the ball back in. Diego will stop at second, giving you first and second with no one out.

Up comes your leftfielder, Al Berico, with the winning run in scoring position. He's ready. Now here's the pitch . . . it's popped up to the right side. Their first baseman calls and makes the catch, one away. That'll bring up your second baseman, Patrick Berry. He hits a ground ball deep in the hole at short. Their shortstop, moving to his right, backhands the ball. With no chance to get the lead runner, he fires to second, two away. That makes it first and third, and brings up your first baseman, Judd Jackson, who swings and misses at strike three. After a promising start to the ninth, you fail to score and we go to extra innings.

No one scores in the 10th. In the top of the 11th, the Protons pick up a run on a walk, a stolen base and an RBI single. They get you out in order in the bottom of the 11th, and you lose, 2-1, in eleven innings.

SCOREBOARD

YOU LOSE,
2–1

73

*T*here are men on second and third, one out, here in the bottom of the seventh. You trail, 5-4. Out comes your pinch runner, Lee Wilcox, to replace Gonzalez at second base. This is an obvious move to try to score the go-ahead run from second on a base hit. And boy, is Wilcox a terror on the base paths. He's got amazing speed, and has stolen 15 bases in 19 attempts this year, an excellent rate of success.

Now we're ready. In steps Rob Burns, your leadoff batter who's hitting a solid .310 with 44 RBIs. The Protons pitcher works from a full windup, now the delivery ... it's a line drive, base hit to left. One run is in to tie the game. Here comes Wilcox. Here's the throw, the slide, the tag ... he's safe!

Well, that piece of strategy worked out beautifully. The slower catcher would never have made it all the way around from second, but Wilcox was able to score to put you up, 6-5. A single and 2 RBIs for Burns brings his total to 46 for the year. Next up is Guy Diego who flies out. Chris Freeman then strikes out to end the inning.

Both teams are quiet in the eighth. In the top of the ninth, John Neff, the Protons first baseman, leads off with a double up the alley in right center. This could be the start of a rally.

he tying run's on second. I've got my ace warmed up in the pen. I think McAndrews has it in him to finish the game, but that last shot was hit pretty hard. I trust McAndrews to finish, and my gut tells me to stick with him. But all they need is a single to get that run home. Maybe bringing in a fresh pitcher to finish out the ninth would be the safest way to go.

Let's see, their leftfielder, Trevor Nelson, is up next. He's a good fastball hitter, but his overall numbers for the year are only so-so. My starter is a finesse artist, but Ron Murphy, my bullpen ace, is a fireballer. I may do better to stay with my cagey starter, to keep Nelson off-balance, instead of trying to blow it by someone who knows how to handle the heat.

▲ To bring in a relief pitcher, turn to page 78

▲ To leave your starter in, turn to page 79

With men at second and third, there's one away here in the bottom of the seventh. You're trailing 5-4, and your centerfielder, Rob Burns, comes up to bat. The runners take their leads. The Protons pitcher will work from a full windup. Here's the pitch . . . it's swung on . . . it's a line drive base hit going into left. One run is in. The man from second base stops at third. You've tied the game, 5-5.

That'll bring up your rookie rightfielder, Guy Diego. The runners take their leads from first and third. Their pitcher works from the stretch. Here's the pitch, and the man on third suddenly charges for home! Diego swings and lines a foul ball into the stands behind third. That was a close call for the runner—that ball could have hit him!

Diego missed the squeeze sign! I can't believe he's still making rookie mistakes like that this late in the season! I was hoping to shock the Protons by calling a squeeze play when they would never been expecting the bunt. I mean, look where they were positioned. Everyone was playing back for the double play, and we have a slow runner on third. It was such a surprise it might have worked. But Diego missed the sign.

We sure were lucky. That ball almost beaned Burnsie. We're also lucky that Diego got a piece of that pitch, with the runner charging home. If he had swung and missed, the runner would have been dead at the plate.

I could come right back with the squeeze again, figuring that this time they'd really be caught off guard. But I'm a little worried that my batter will miss the sign again. Also, with only one away, the man from third could score on a fly ball too.

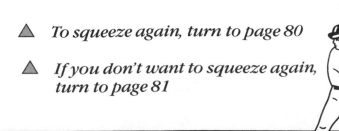

▲ *To squeeze again, turn to page 80*

▲ *If you don't want to squeeze again, turn to page 81*

*T*here's a man on second and nobody out here in the top of the ninth. Here comes the manager out to the mound. That'll be all for McAndrews. In from the bullpen trots Ron Murphy, the lefty relief ace. He's had a great season and looks like a strong candidate for Fireman of the Year honors. His record is 6-1 with a 1.96 ERA and 88 strikeouts; in 94 innings of relief he's allowed only 40 walks. He's a power guy. He'll try to blow them away with his 90-plus-miles-per-hour fastball.

Murphy will face a good fastball hitter, however, in the Protons leftfielder, Trevor Nelson. He works from the stretch, checks the runner at second, now the pitch . . . the fastball is swung on and crushed to rightfield, no doubt about this one, it's out of here! This is a classic example of a good fastball hitter getting hold of a blazer and putting power to power. The Protons grab the lead, 7-6.

Murphy gets the next three batters out to retire the side, but you fail to score in the bottom of the ninth and lose, 7-6.

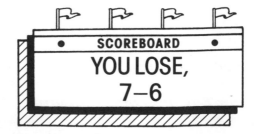

SCOREBOARD

YOU LOSE,
7–6

They've got a man on second, nobody out here in the top of the ninth. At the plate is the Protons left-fielder, Trevor Nelson. McAndrews works from the stretch. He checks the runner, now he's ready, here's the pitch ... it's popped up on the left side of the infield. Your shortstop calls and makes the catch, one away.

That brings up their catcher, Nick Klein. McAndrews stops at the belt, looks toward second, now the delivery ... it's a ground ball to second, fielded on an easy hop by your second baseman. He flips to first, two down. The runner on second, Neff, moves to third.

It'll be up to their shortstop, Walker Smith, to get the tying run home.

McAndrews will go back to the full windup with the runner on third. He looks in for the sign from the catcher, and shakes off a couple. Now he's got one he likes. McAndrews is into his motion, now the pitch ... it's a fly ball to leftfield, this could be trouble, your left-fielder races toward the line and ... makes the catch! A running shoestring grab ends the ball game. You hold on to win, 6-5, and move into the playoffs!

SCOREBOARD

YOU WIN,
6–5!

*I*t's a 5-5 ball game with one away in the bottom of the seventh. Guy Diego steps back into the box after missing that squeeze sign. Now he takes a good long look down to the coaching box at third. He's ready. The Protons pitcher works from the stretch. The runners take their lead from first and third. Here's the pitch ... they're trying the squeeze again! Here comes the runner from third. The pitch is bunted, but it's hit too hard, right back to the pitcher. He flips to home for the easy out at the plate, and the catcher fires to first for the double play. I think that move caught everyone by surprise. A well-executed bunt might have gotten the run home, but Diego pushed it too hard, resulting in a double play to end the inning.

No one scores in the eighth or ninth, and we go to extra innings. In the top of the 10th, the Protons pick up a run on a solo homer by their red-hot first baseman to take the lead, 6-5. You fail to score in the bottom of the 10th, and lose, 6-5.

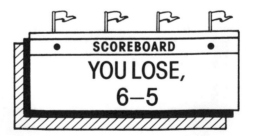

• SCOREBOARD •

YOU LOSE,
6–5

T here are men at first and third, with one out here in the bottom of the seventh, and a one-strike count on your rightfielder, Guy Diego. The game's tied 5-5. On the last pitch the squeeze was called, but Diego missed the sign. Let's see what the manager calls here. Your runners lead from first and third. Wilson is into his stretch, now the pitch ... no squeeze this time. The pitch is swung on and hit to left, not very deep. This ball is going to be caught for the second out.

I t's not too deep, and my man on third isn't that fast. Other people would say that means this is a crazy time to even *think* of having him tag up. But I think it might be worth taking a chance. We might draw a bad throw and get the go-ahead run home. Besides, if I don't send him, there are two outs and I could strand the go-ahead run on third. I'm going to signal my third base coach before the ball is caught so he knows what to do. My left hand pulls my right ear twice, then my right hand taps the brim of my cap once.

▲ *To have the man on third stay, turn to page 82*

▲ *To have the man on third tag up, turn to page 83*

he ball is caught, and the man on third holds. Now there are two down. That brings up your third baseman, Chris Freeman, facing a first-and-third situation in this 5-5 game. Wilson works from the stretch, steps off, throws to first . . . not in time. Now the runners take their leads again. Wilson is at the belt, now the delivery . . . it's swung on and hit deep to right. Their rightfielder, Luis Acosta, races to the wall. This could be over his head. He leaps . . . and makes the catch! Oh, what a spectacular grab by Acosta. With his back to home plate and the ball arcing over his head, he leaped and made the one-handed catch, hit the ground and held onto the ball. That looked like an extra-base hit for sure. That catch was a real game-saver. The inning is over and the game is still tied, 5-5.

No one scores in the eighth. In the top of the ninth the Protons second baseman, Malley, leads off with a walk. Their centerfielder, Carlos Ferrer, is up next, and he hits a towering drive deep to center that is out of here! A monster two-run home run gives them the lead, 7-5. You fail to score in the bottom of the ninth and lose, 7-5.

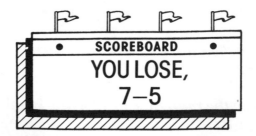

SCOREBOARD
YOU LOSE,
7–5

The ball is caught for the second out. The runner on third is tagging, and he breaks for the plate! Here comes the throw in from left, they may get the slow runner . . . no, the throw is off line. It comes in on the wrong side of the plate. The Protons catcher, Nick Klein, must get the ball and bring it all the way across the plate to make the tag, which is not in time to get the runner. A good throw would probably have had him, but because Klein had to shift his balance to get to the ball, then shift back, he had to try for a swiping tag, rather than setting himself up to block the plate. So the run scores on a gutsy gamble. You take back the lead, 6-5. Your third baseman grounds out to short to end the inning, but you have regained the lead in this back-and-forth game.

You bring in Ron Murphy, your lefty relief ace—who is 6-1, with a 1.96 ERA and 88 strikeouts in 94 innings—to face them in the eighth and ninth. In the eighth he gets out the side in order. In the ninth, he gives up base hits to their catcher and shortstop, but then gets a pinch hitter to fly out to right and strikes out the second baseman and centerfielder to end the ball game. You win, 6-5, to make it into the playoffs.

SCOREBOARD

YOU WIN,
6–5!

*I*t's the bottom of the 12th, two men out. You trail by one, 4-3. Guy Diego has a 2-and-1 count on him, and Burns is on first. The runner takes his lead. The Protons pitcher comes to the one-second stop at the belt, checks the runner, now here comes the pitch. There goes Burns trying to steal second!

The pitch is swung on and lined into the gap in right center. Burns is rounding second, he'll get to third easily. The ball gets between the two outfielders and rolls all the way to the wall. The runner is being waved around. The throw comes in to the cutoff man, but they won't get him. Guy Diego pulls into second with a double, and Burns scores all the way from first. You've tied it up again, 4-4.

That brings up your third baseman, Chris Freeman with the go-ahead run in scoring position. However, it's a wasted opportunity as Freeman strikes out to end the inning.

No one scores in the 13th. In the bottom of the 14th, your shortstop, John Miner, singles. The next two batters strike out and fly out, bringing up Burns again.

*T*he 14th inning! **We'll be here all night if I don't make something happen. Still, the fans are getting their money's worth. This is some ballgame.**

Even though there are two outs, I'd like to send Miner on a straight steal to get him down into scoring position. Burns is one of my most reliable hitters. If I can get Miner to second, there's a better than average chance he'd run around with the winning run. But Miner only has average speed. He's stolen just once in three attempts in the short timc hc's been up with the big club. And if he doesn't make it, then I've taken the winning run off the bases and ended the inning. If I don't get things going now, though, I may not get another chance.

▲ *If you don't want to attempt a steal, turn to page 87*

▲ *To attempt a steal, turn to page 89*

You're down to your final out, trailing 4-3 in the bottom of the 12th. Burns is on first and a 2-and-1 count on Guy Diego. The Protons pitcher goes into his motion, he checks the runner at first, now the pitch . . . it's swung on and fouled off, the count goes to 2 and 2. Burns was not going with the pitch. Their pitcher looks in for his sign. Now he's ready. The runner takes his lead from first. The pitcher comes set. Now the pitch . . . it's in there for a called strike three! The game is over. You lose in 12, by a score of 4-3.

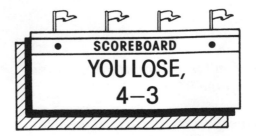

SCOREBOARD

YOU LOSE,
4–3

*T*here are two men away in the bottom of the 14th. Rob Burns is at bat with John Miner on first and the score tied, 4–4. Wilson is into his motion, now the pitch . . . it's a ground ball back past the pitcher into center for a base hit. Miner wasn't moving with the pitch, and he has to stop at second.

That'll bring up your rightfielder, Guy Diego. The runners take their leads, the Protons pitcher works from the stretch. Here's the pitch . . . it's a fly ball to straightaway center; this should be the inning. Their centerfielder settles under it, makes the catch, and we go to the 15th.

Their second baseman, Steve Malley, leads the inning off with a groundout to third. That brings up Carlos Ferrer, the centerfielder, who hits a line drive to left for a base hit. Next up is the third baseman, Sam Alexander. Your pitcher will work from the stretch. He comes to the stop, checks the runner at first, now delivers. The ball's hit right down the first-base line, the ump says fair! It's rolling toward the stands. Your rightfielder was playing way over and he has to run a long way to get there, now—wait a minute! A fan has reached out and grabbed the ball. They'll have to rule this a ground-rule double, but—what's this? I don't believe it. The umpire is ruling that if the fan had *not* touched the ball, it would have bounced into the right-field corner, and with your rightfielder playing so far over, the man on first would have been able to score. They're sending him home with the go-ahead run here in the 15th.

Here you come out of the dugout, and you're

screaming at the umps. Here you are, in your home park, and one of your own fans, more concerned about getting a souvenir than about seeing his team win, grabs the ball, forcing the umps to rule that the go-ahead run would have scored. Perhaps it might have, but if the fan hadn't interfered, you might have at least had a shot at a play.

Now they've ejected you from the game! You're out of the game, and the run will stand.

You get out of the inning but fail to score in the bottom of the 15th, and lose, 5–4, on a controversial call that they'll be talking about all winter.

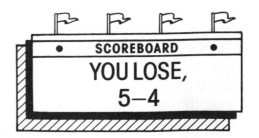

Burns will bat with two down in the 14th and John Miner on first in this 4–4 tie. The runner takes his lead. The Protons pitcher stops at the belt, checks the runner, now throws over, but the rookie shortstop gets back in time. The pitcher comes set again. Here's the pitch and the runner goes, trying to steal second. Burns takes the pitch. Here's the throw by their catcher ... it's off line, and it takes a good play by their second baseman to stop the ball from going into centerfield and allowing Miner to move all the way to third. A stolen base on a straight steal puts the winning run into scoring position with two down. Your centerfielder's still at bat.

Their pitcher is ready, he's got his sign. He stops at the belt, glances toward Miner at second, here's the pitch ... it's a line drive to leftfield for a base hit. The runner rounds third. Their leftfielder sets and fires his throw to the plate. It'll be close, here's the slide, the tag ... he's safe! You win! In the bottom of the 14th you pick up the winning run on some heads-up baserunning by your rookie shortstop to take the game 5–4 and move into the playoffs.

• SCOREBOARD •

YOU WIN,
5–4!

About the Author

Michael Teitelbaum was born and raised in Brooklyn, N.Y. He currently lives with his wife in Manhattan, where for the past 12 years he has been a writer and editor of children's books and periodicals. He has written and edited books and magazines based on Mickey Mouse, Bugs Bunny, Fraggle Rock, The Muppets, Sesame Street, Alvin and the Chipmunks, The Little Mermaid, The Rescuers Down Under, Winnie-the-Pooh, The Tawny Scrawny Lion, DuckTales, Gremlins (I & II), Chip N' Dale, Ghostbusters, The Jetsons and *An American Tail,* to name a few. Most recently he was editor of *DuckTales* magazine and *The Real Ghostbusters* magazine. His first original story, *But You're a Duck!* was published in 1990 as a Little Golden Book. He is a longtime fan of the New York Mets and the New York Knicks, and is still a Green Bay Packer fan (don't ask why!).

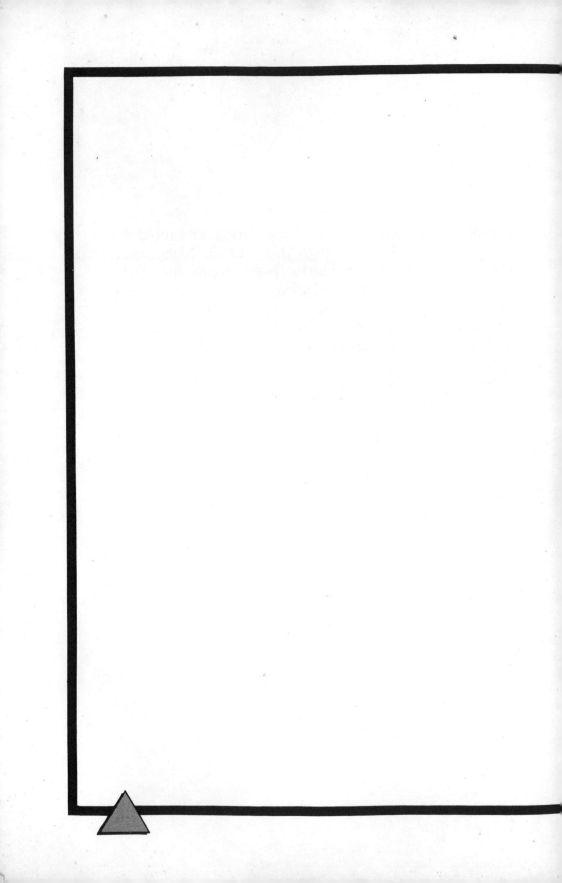